In the Footsteps of Explorers

Henry Hudson

Seeking the Northwest Passage

Carrie Gleason

 Crabtree Publishing Company

www.crabtreebooks.com

Crabtree Publishing Company
www.crabtreebooks.com

For Charlotte and back-to-school.

Coordinating editor: Ellen Rodger
Project editor: Rachel Eagen
Editor: Adrianna Morganelli
Proofreader: Michele Collins
Design and production coordinator: Rosie Gowsell
Cover design and production assistance: Samara Parent
Art direction: Rob MacGregor
Scanning technician: Arlene Arch-Wilson
Photo research: Allison Napier

Consultant: Tracey L. Neikirk, Museum Educator, The Mariners' Museum

Photo Credits: Brian and Cherry Alexander/ Photo Researchers, Inc.: p. 25; The Art Archive: p. 26; Bettmann/ CORBIS: p. 13, p. 28; Brooklyn Museum of Art/ Corbis: p. 31 (top); Jason Burke; Eye Ubiquitous/ Corbis: p. 17 (top); Girdudon/ Art Resource, NY: p. 7 (bottom); George D. Lepp/ Photo Researchers, Inc.: p. 21 (bottom); Erich Lessing/ Art Resource, NY: p. 7 (top); North Wind/ North Wind Picture Archives: p. 8-9, p. 14-15, p. 19, p. 20, p. 29; Onne van der Wal/ Corbis: p. 11; Gianni Dagli Orti/ Corbis: p. 27 (top); Tate Gallery, London/ Art Resource, NY: cover, p. 23; Underwood & Underwood/ Corbis: p. 30.

Illustrations: Lauren Fast: p. 4, p. 6; David Wysotski: pp. 16-17

Cartography: Jim Chernishenko: p. 10, p. 12, p. 21

Cover: The Last Voyage of Henry Hudson is an oil painting by John Collier. The painting, exhibited in 1881, depicts a defeated Henry Hudson, his son John, and a sick crew member after they were set afloat in the Arctic by the crew of Hudson's ship, the *Half Moon*.

Title page: Henry Hudson traveled northeast, then northwest, looking for a route to Asia from Europe.

Sidebar icon: Some of Hudson's crew reported that they saw mysterious creatures, such as mermaids and strange fish, swimming in the waters of the uncharted Arctic.

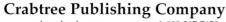

Crabtree Publishing Company
www.crabtreebooks.com   1-800-387-7650

Cataloging-in-Publication Data
Gleason, Carrie, 1973-
    Henry Hudson : seeking the Northwest Passage / written by Carrie Gleason.
       p. cm. -- (In the footsteps of explorers)
    Includes index.
    ISBN-13: 978-0-7787-2408-7 (rlb)
    ISBN-10: 0-7787-2408-5 (rlb)
    ISBN-13: 978-0-7787-2444-5 (pbk)
    ISBN-10: 0-7787-2444-1 (pbk)
  1. Hudson, Henry, d. 1611--Travel--Juvenile literature. 2. America--Discovery and exploration--English--Juvenile literature. 3. Explorers--America--Biography--Juvenile literature. 4. Explorers--Great Britain--Biography--Juvenile literature. I. Title. II. Series.
    E129.H8G58 2005
    910'.92--dc22
                            2005001083
                            LC

**Published in
the United States**
PMB 16A
350 Fifth Ave.
Suite 3308
New York, NY
10118

**Published
in Canada**
616 Welland Ave.
St. Catharines
Ontario, Canada
L2M 5V6

**Published in the
United Kingdom**
73 Lime Walk
Headington
Oxford
0X3 7AD
United Kingdom

**Published
in Australia**
386 Mt. Alexander Rd.
Ascot Vale (Melbourne)
V1C 3032

Contents

Northern Wish

Henry Hudson was an English explorer who sailed the icy waters of the Arctic. He was looking for a passage that would allow ships to reach Asia from Europe. Hudson made many attempts to voyage through the Arctic, but he never accomplished his goal.

Early Life

No written records of Henry Hudson's early life exist today. Historians believe that Hudson was born in England sometime between 1565 and 1570. They also believe Hudson was a crew member on the early Arctic voyages of English explorer John Davis. Henry Hudson's grandfather may have been one of the founders of the Muscovy Company, the **merchant company** that paid for Hudson's first two voyages.

Determination and Death

Despite threats of **mutiny**, and of losing the **financial support** of the merchant companies that funded his voyages, Hudson was determined to find a passage. On his last voyage, his crew feared that Hudson was leading them all to a certain death in the Arctic. They mutinied, and set Hudson and a few loyal crew members to drift in a small boat in Hudson Bay. Hudson was never heard from again.

(above) Henry Hudson weathered the fierce snowstorms and icebergs of the North as he tried to find a passage to Asia from Europe. Traveling northeast, then northwest, Hudson died before making a successful voyage.

In the Words of...

Led by the **first mate**, Hudson, his teenaged son, John, and some others, were abandoned in Hudson Bay with few supplies. The mutiny was recorded in the journal of Abacuk Prickett, one of the crew members onboard.

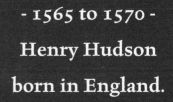

"...John Thomas and Bennet stood in front of him [Hudson]. He asked them what they meant by this? They told him he would know when he was in the shallop [ship's boat]. ... The master [Hudson] called to the carpenter and told him that he was bound. ... Then the shallop was brought up to the ship's side, and the poor, sick and lame men were made to get out of their cabins and into the shallop. They sailed out of the ice with the shallop tied fast to its stern, and when they were well out, they cut her adrift. We stayed here that night and the best part of the next day, never seeing the shallop then, or ever after."

(right) Hudson and his crew shot a walrus for food in the harsh Arctic waters.

- 1565 to 1570 -
Henry Hudson born in England.

- 1607 -
Hudson's first voyage.

- 1608 to 1610 -
Hudson makes three more voyages to try to find a passage.

- 1611 -
Hudson set adrift in small boat on Hudson Bay and is never heard from again.

- 1488 -
Bartolomeu Dias becomes the first European to sail around the Cape of Good Hope, the southernmost tip of Africa.

- 1492 -
Italian explorer Christopher Columbus (above) sails across the Atlantic Ocean, where he finds present-day Bahamas.

- 1498 -
Vasco da Gama becomes the first European to sail from Europe to India.

Age of Exploration

The quest for a northern passage to Asia filled the hopes of English merchants around 1600. Until then, Portuguese sailors had dominated trade routes to India, China, and the Spice Islands. Merchants desired trade goods, such as spices, gold, silk, and porcelain.

Portuguese Explorers

Portuguese explorers discovered a sea route around the southern tip of Africa to India and the Spice Islands. Portuguese merchants grew wealthy exploring the coasts of Africa. They brought pepper, ivory, gold, salt, and Africans to be sold as slaves, back to Europe. Trading posts were set up as far away as Japan. Portuguese merchants held exclusive rights to trade with locals at the trading posts. The sailors on merchant ships fiercely defended their trading posts and trade route by attacking ships from other European countries that sailed into them.

(right) Europeans wanted spices, such as pepper, cloves, and cinnamon to season their food. The desire for spices fueled the spice trade.

(above) A flotilla of the Dutch East India Company around 1675. A group of merchants formed the company to break the Portuguese monopoly of the spice trade.

The Dutch

From Portuguese ports, Dutch ships carried the valuable Asian goods to cities in northern Europe. The Dutch built up a large **merchant fleet** of fast ships with experienced crew. The Dutch began attacking the Portuguese ships and eventually became the leader in trade. The Dutch East India Company was a merchant company formed in 1602. Its purpose was to control trade with Asia, and to fight the enemies of the Netherlands, including Spain and Portugal.

(right) European merchants wanted to reach Asia so they could sell Asian spices and trade goods to wealthy Europeans.

Quest for Passage

Portugal and the Netherlands battled for control over the southern trade route around the tip of Africa to Asia. Other European countries tried to find a new route. Explorers looked for a sea route to Asia, which they called the Northwest Passage.

In the Works

Geographers believed that a passage to Asia would be shorter and easier if ships sailed across the North Pole. At the time, no European had ever been to the North Pole, so they did not know that the Arctic is a permanently frozen ocean. Scholars wrote books that claimed ships could cross the North Pole because the sun shines continuously there for a few months of the year. To them, this meant that the Arctic was a warm ocean that only froze over in winter.

The Quest Begins

In 1587, English explorer John Davis led an expedition to find the Northwest Passage. The expedition was paid for by merchants in England. Between the present-day countries of Greenland and Canada, Davis and his crew sailed by a **channel** filled with whirlpools and floating ice. Davis did not try to enter the channel, because he had to turn back to England before winter arrived. He named the channel the Furious Overfall.

(background) Hudson and his crew sailed further north than any other Europeans. They were unprepared for the bitter cold of the Arctic, and did not know when they would return home.

The Merchant Companies

Merchant companies, or chartered companies, were groups of merchants who were granted a charter, or special permission, from a king or queen. This allowed them to be the only merchants in their country to control one whole area of trade. Merchant companies explored new lands to find new trade items and new people to trade with. They even set up colonies in lands they discovered. The Muscovy Company, in England, was started in the 1550s to find a Northeast Passage to Asia. Attempts by explorers to find a passage led to trade links with Russia.

(above) Merchant ships from England carried wool to be traded in Russia.

To the Arctic

In 1607, The Muscovy Company hired Henry Hudson to find a passage to Asia. Hudson read many books by geographers who claimed the north was navigable. He believed the shortest route would cross over the North Pole. Hudson left England aboard the *Hopewell*.

First Voyage

Hudson sailed northwest by the Faroe Islands and Greenland, where he ran into thick fog and rain that froze on the ship's deck. After being at sea for six weeks, Hudson spotted the mountains of Greenland to the west. The crew sailed along the coast of Greenland, mapping it as they went. The ship changed **course** and turned toward the Spitsbergen Islands after they ran into pack ice. Sailing through the islands for several weeks, the crew saw many seals and walruses and sailed into a bay where there were thousands of whales. Hudson named the place Whales Bay.

(above) On the Spitsbergen Islands, the crew found antlers, geese, and clear spring water. These discoveries made Hudson think the North Pole was going to be as mild as the island climate.

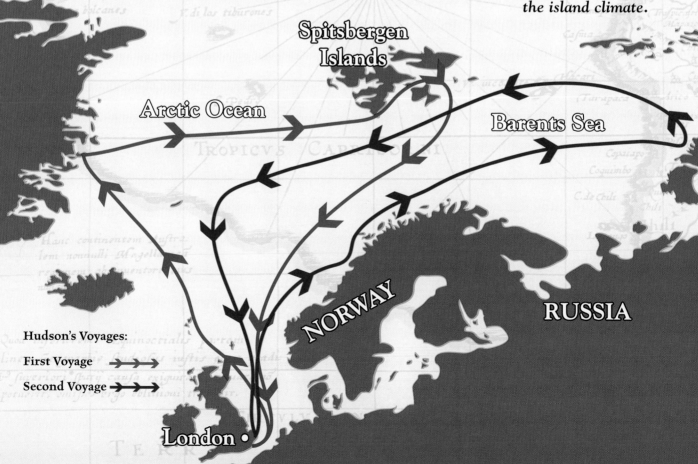

Spitsbergen Islands

Arctic Ocean

Barents Sea

NORWAY

RUSSIA

Hudson's Voyages:

First Voyage →→→

Second Voyage →→→

London •

Second Voyage

Hudson figured that his mistake on the first voyage had been to try to sail directly over the North Pole. For his second attempt, Hudson looked for a Northeast Passage along the northern coast of Russia. Again aboard the *Hopewell*, Hudson sailed from England to the northern coast of Norway. The ship entered the Barents Sea and reached the island of Novaya Zemlya. Hudson sailed along the west coast of the island, trying to find a waterway that would allow passage to the Kara Sea on the other side. When the weather turned stormy, Hudson sailed back to England. After three and a half months at sea, Hudson and his crew had sailed further north than any other Europeans. They came within 600 miles (966 kilometers) of the North Pole. Upon his return to England, the Muscovy Company fired Hudson because they considered his voyage a failure.

(above) The Spitsbergen Islands make up a mountainous archipelago, or group of islands, north of present-day Norway.

- May 1, 1607 -
Hudson leaves England with eleven crew members.

- September 15, 1607 -
Hudson and crew return to England.

- April 22, 1608 -
Hudson departs England on a second voyage with fourteen crew members.

- August 7, 1608 -
Hudson signs agreement to take crew back to England.

- August 26, 1608 -
Hudson and crew return to England.

Hudson in America

The Muscovy Company refused to pay for any more of Hudson's voyages after his failure to find a Northeast Passage. Hudson went to the Dutch East India Company in Amsterdam to ask them for funds.

The Journey Begins

After getting funds from the Dutch, Hudson and his crew left Amsterdam for Novaya Zemlya aboard the *Half Moon*. The contract that Hudson had signed stated that he was to search for a Northeast Passage. Within a month, Hudson proposed to the crew that they head to North America to escape the harsh Arctic cold. The crew agreed, and they sailed across the Atlantic Ocean until they reached present-day Maine. Hudson had disobeyed his orders by steering off course.

Up the Hudson River

Hudson sailed as far south as the **Virginia colony** at Chesapeake Bay. From there, Hudson turned his ship north and sailed up the coast, looking for a passage. The *Half Moon* reached the mouth of the Hudson River, in what is now New York state. Earlier explorers to North America had seen the river, but no European had entered it. As Hudson sailed up the river, he noted that it became increasingly shallow, proving it was not the passage to Asia.

(above) Hudson first anchored off Penobscot Bay, in present-day Maine. While repairing a damaged mast, his crew caught and ate lobster.

NORTH AMERICA

Penobscot Bay

Hudson River

Atlantic Ocean

Chesapeake Bay

Hudson's Third Voyage →→→

Back to the Ocean

Once the ship reached the open ocean, Hudson held a meeting with his officers and it was decided they would return home. When they arrived in England, Hudson sent word to the Dutch East India Company of the river he had found that led to the interior of North America. When England's King James I heard this, he had Hudson arrested. The king and the merchants of London were furious because all that Hudson had discovered now belonged to the Dutch, because they had paid for the voyage. The English people were outraged at Hudson's arrest. It was not against any English law to sail under another country's flag. The king was convinced to free Hudson and to allow him to sail for England.

(below) Hudson traded furs with native North Americans.

- April 6, 1609 -

Beginning of third voyage.

- July 14, 1609 -

Half Moon reaches coast of Maine.

- July 18, 1609 -

Hudson first sets foot on North America.

- September 3, 1609 -

Enters mouth of the Hudson River.

- November 7, 1609 -
Half Moon reaches England.

Deadly Contact

When Henry Hudson explored the Hudson River, he found the native people who had lived there for thousands of years. The journals written by Hudson and his crew tell that the Europeans did not trust the natives they met.

The Penobscot Natives

The first native peoples Hudson met were the Penobscot, when he landed in what is now Maine. The Penobscot survived by hunting animals, such as bears and moose, by growing crops in fields, especially corn, by fishing with nets and spears in rivers, and by catching clams, lobsters, and crabs in the Atlantic Ocean. When Hudson and his crew reached Penobscot Bay, they traded their wool nightshirts for native furs.

Turn of the Tide

At first, Hudson and his crew had peaceful contact with the Penobscot. Then, Hudson's first mate, Robert Juet, and another crew member, stole native canoes and paddled to their camp. There, the crew charged with their muskets and stole furs, deerskin capes, moccasins, and clothing from the natives. The crew feared that if they had not attacked the native camp first, then the natives would have attacked them.

Contact with the Lenape

After sailing along the coast of North America to what is now New York, Hudson entered into territory that belonged to the Lenape native peoples. The Lenape paddled out in their canoes to trade tobacco, knives, and beads with Hudson and his crew. The next day, Hudson sent some of his crew out to explore the river in the ship's boat. The Lenape attacked the men and one of the crew was killed when an arrow was shot through his neck. After the attack, two canoes carrying natives with bows and arrows approached the ship. The crew took two of the Lenape hostage, believing that they would be safe from any future attacks because of the hostages onboard. Further up the river, the two hostages escaped by prying the boards off the **porthole**, wiggling out, and swimming to shore.

(above) Native peoples made clothing from deer and moose hide. They traded for beads to decorate clothing.

Contact with the Mahican

The Mahicans also lived on the Hudson River. Hudson and his crew were the first Europeans the Mahicans had come into contact with. Hudson was invited to feast with the Mahican chief. The meal they ate included sweet corn, pigeon, dog, and a **mash** made from tree bark and berries. Hudson admired the Mahican's skills as hunters, builders, fishers, and farmers.

(background) Depiction of Hudson arriving in North America. Some native groups, such as the Lenape, that Hudson met had already had contact with Europeans, and were wary of them. Others, such as the Mahicans, had never met Europeans and were friendlier.

Life at Sea

Crew members on ships of exploration faced many hardships. Long voyages to unknown lands meant rough weather, food shortages, and the fear of attack by natives.

At Home at Sea

Once at sea, the ship's crew slept in cramped quarters in the forecastle, or forward part of the ship, with the stored gear and ropes. Hammocks were strung from wall to wall and served as beds. The captain of the ship had his own cabin, which was only large enough for a bed and a place to look at charts and maps.

(below) Barrels stored onboard contained water, ale, salt, dried meat and vegetables, and cheese. The water soon turned green and could not be drunk. The salt was used to preserve fish caught at sea.

Corn Bread

When Hudson reached North America, he was introduced to corn, which he called turkish wheat. Native peoples made bread using ground corn as flour. Here is a modern-day recipe for corn bread.

Ingredients:

1 1/2 cups cornmeal

1/2 cup flour

2 teaspoons baking powder

1/2 teaspoon salt

2 tablespoons sugar

2 eggs

1 cup buttermilk

3 tablespoons vegetable oil

Directions:

1. Preheat oven to 400°F. Grease a small square baking pan and heat in oven.

2. In a large bowl, mix together the cornmeal, flour, baking powder, salt, and sugar.

3. In a separate bowl, beat eggs, add buttermilk and oil. Pour wet ingredients into dry, and stir to mix.

4. Carefully remove heated pan from oven. Pour in batter. Bake for 20-30 minutes.

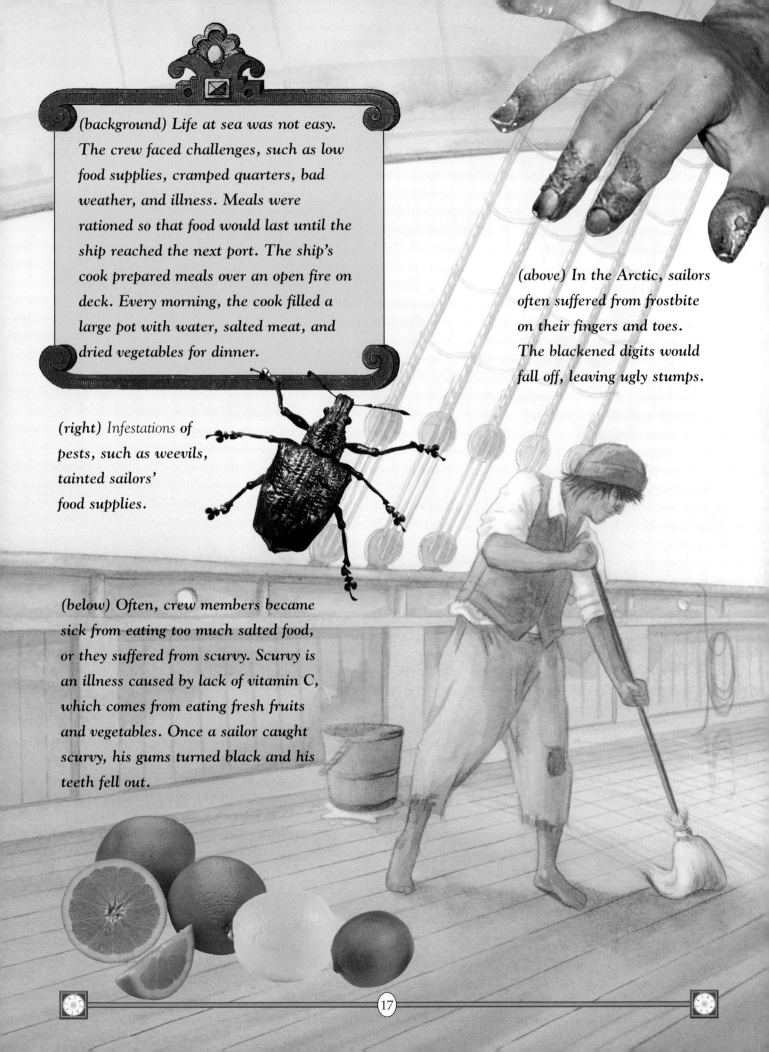

(background) Life at sea was not easy. The crew faced challenges, such as low food supplies, cramped quarters, bad weather, and illness. Meals were rationed so that food would last until the ship reached the next port. The ship's cook prepared meals over an open fire on deck. Every morning, the cook filled a large pot with water, salted meat, and dried vegetables for dinner.

(above) In the Arctic, sailors often suffered from frostbite on their fingers and toes. The blackened digits would fall off, leaving ugly stumps.

(right) Infestations of pests, such as weevils, tainted sailors' food supplies.

(below) Often, crew members became sick from eating too much salted food, or they suffered from scurvy. Scurvy is an illness caused by lack of vitamin C, which comes from eating fresh fruits and vegetables. Once a sailor caught scurvy, his gums turned black and his teeth fell out.

Ready the Ships!

The ships used by explorers in the 1600s were a lot smaller than those used today. They were made from wood and had tall sails that provided power only when the wind blew.

The Hopewell, Half Moon, and Discovery

The ship for Hudson's first and second voyages, called the *Hopewell*, was from the Muscovy Company. It was a bark, which was a ship with three wooden masts. The *Hopewell* was made for sailing on calm waters, and had trouble with the rough waves of the Arctic Ocean.

Hudson's third voyage was aboard a two-masted Dutch trading ship called the *Half Moon*. The *Half Moon* was a broad, flat-bottomed boat built to sail through shallow coastal waters.

The *Discovery* was the ship Hudson used on his fourth voyage. At 65 feet (20 meters) it was larger than any other of Hudson's ships. The *Discovery* had already made a voyage to the Canadian Arctic where the crew on its first voyage mutinied.

Maps and Charts

Maps and charts of the areas Hudson explored were based on descriptions told by fishermen and sailors to mapmakers at the time. Explorers did not really know what to expect on their voyages. Mapmakers back in Europe made new maps based on the journals and reports made by explorers when they returned home. As explorers traveled, they noted the physical landscape of a place and took measurements of the sea depth using a piece of lead tied to a rope.

- Navigation -

To navigate a ship at sea, explorers used a process called dead reckoning. In dead reckoning, a ship's course, or path, was calculated using the measurement of the direction the ship was traveling in, the time it took to get there, and the speed it was traveling at.

(background) An illustration of Hudson's ship, the Half Moon, on New York's Hudson River, in 1609. Larger ships also carried smaller boats, which were used to explore smaller streams and rivers.

Mutiny!

From the beginning of Hudson's fourth voyage, there were troubles with the crew. Hudson was a determined explorer, but a poor leader. This weakness as a leader lead to his death.

At Sea

Hudson's final voyage was paid for by merchants in London who formed a company called the Company of Gentlemen. They hired Hudson to find the elusive Northwest Passage. Hudson sailed the *Discovery* northwest, navigating around icebergs and through arctic storms until he reached an area of surging tides, ice floes, and thick fog called the Furious Overfall.

Troubles Brewing

Hudson had trouble controlling his crew and they lost confidence in him. One sailor beat up another sailor, and was not punished. Hudson's first mate, Robert Juet, was openly rebellious. The crew was terrified to sail through Furious Overfall, but Hudson believed it lead to Asia. The crew begged Hudson to turn back, but he refused. The ship entered Hudson Bay, then James Bay where Hudson sailed back and forth looking for the passage.

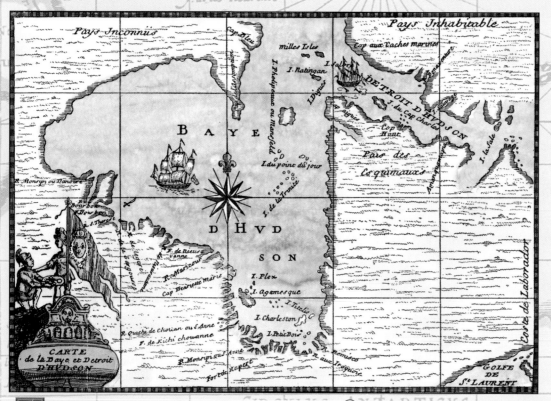

(left) The cold bay where Hudson was set adrift is now called Hudson's Bay, in northern Canada. The Hudson Strait, or Furious Overfall, connected the bay to the Atlantic.

KALAALLIT NUNAAT
(GREENLAND)

Arctic Ocean

Hudson
Bay

Hudson
Strait

London •

NORTH
AMERICA

Hudson's Fourth Voyage →→→

Juet on Trial

While Hudson focused on finding the Northwest Passage, Juet turned the crew against Hudson. He told them that the ship was lost and that Hudson's decisions meant death for them all. Juet threatened to **seize** the ship and head back to England. This time, Hudson put Juet on trial for mutiny. He gave his position as first mate to another crew member. This caused a split in loyalties among the crew; half were loyal to Hudson, and the other half believed Juet. Juet knew that if they ever did return to England, he was finished as a sailor and he might even be hanged. He began to **conspire** with those loyal to him.

Angering the Crew

By the time winter approached, the crew's eight months of rations were running out. Trapped in ice, they had no choice but to spend the winter in the bay. Hudson offered money to anyone who killed wild bird or game. The ship's gunner, **John Williams**, took the challenge and froze to death trying. Usually, when a crew member died, his belongings were sold to other crew members and the money was given to the dead crew member's family. Hudson, however, offered the coat to another crew member first.

Winter in the North

Hudson decided that they needed a shelter built on shore to spend the winter. He told the ship's carpenter to build the shelter. The carpenter refused to leave the ship. Hudson got angry and threatened to hang him. Eventually, a shelter was built and the crew spent seven and a half months stranded and starving in the arctic winter. Hudson suspected the crew of **hoarding** food and had their belongings searched. The crew also suspected Hudson of hoarding food for himself and those loyal to him.

Mutiny!

By late spring, the ice thawed and the ship was freed. Hudson ordered that they set sail for England, but he steered the ship west. The crew feared that they were not heading home. On June 24, 1611, as Hudson emerged from his cabin, three men, led by Juet, grabbed him. The men tied Hudson's hands and feet and put him into the ship's boat. The boat was towed out to open sea and then cut free. Henry Hudson was never seen again.

The Return Voyage

The mutineers searched Hudson's cabin and found biscuits, grain, and beer. Even with these supplies, the crew did not have enough food to get them back to England. They were too weak and the leader of the mutiny, Juet, starved to death on the way home. When they finally reached Ireland, they bought food with the ship's equipment. By the time they reached England, only eight crew members survived.

(background) Crew members loyal to Hudson, his son, John, and those that were ill, were put on the boat with him. The only supplies they had were some tools, a gun, and some grain. The boat was towed toward open water, then cut loose.

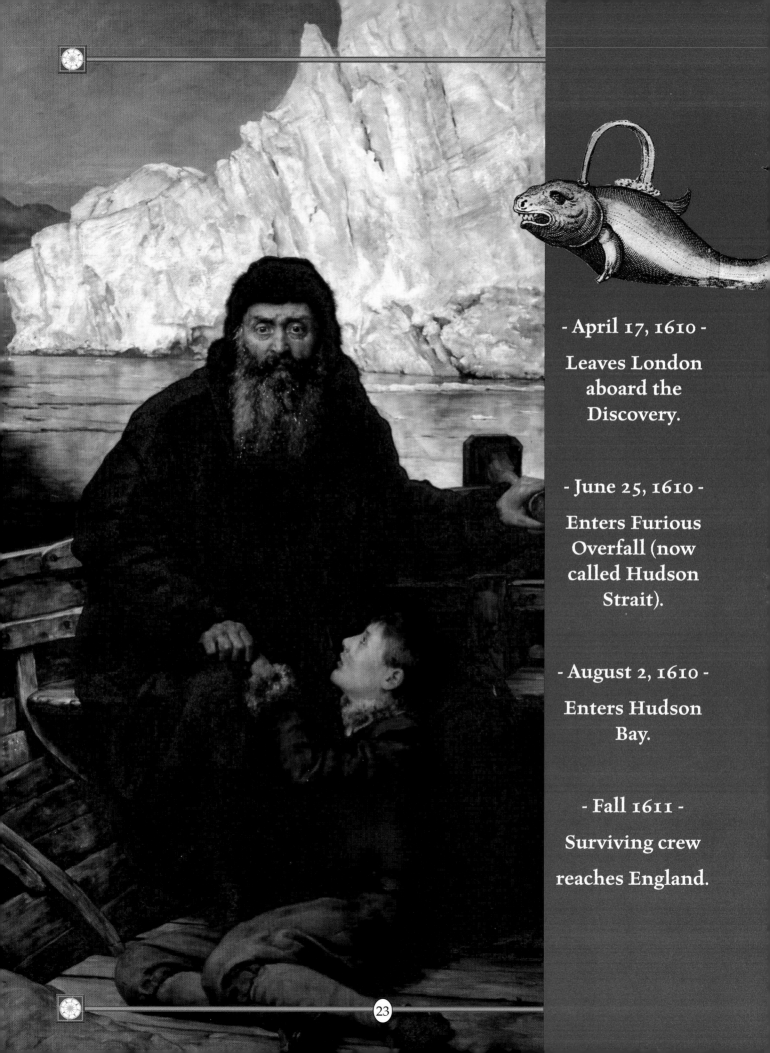

- April 17, 1610 -

Leaves London aboard the Discovery.

- June 25, 1610 -

Enters Furious Overfall (now called Hudson Strait).

- August 2, 1610 -

Enters Hudson Bay.

- Fall 1611 -

Surviving crew reaches England.

Arctic Survival

Hudson and his crew spent one winter stranded in the cold Canadian subarctic. Native peoples who lived in the subarctic, such as the Cree, knew how to survive the long winters. Further north, at the top of Hudson Bay, a group of native peoples called the Inuit had adapted to life in the even more severe Arctic climate.

Cree

The Cree were a native group that lived along the borders of present-day James Bay, where Hudson and his crew spent the winter of 1610. To survive, the Cree lived in tents covered with animal hides or the bark of birch trees. In winter, as food became scarce, the Cree hunted small animals, such as hare, and ate the meat they had preserved for the winter.

Fiery Trade

While stranded over the winter in James Bay, Hudson and his crew were approached by a Cree man. He traded his beaver and deerskins for the crew's knives. Hudson used simple sign language to ask the man to bring the crew food. The Cree man did not return, so Hudson set off to find him. Hudson found the camp and tried to approach. As he neared, the natives set fire to the trees around their camp to keep Hudson out.

(above) The Cree, who lived around James Bay, hunted large animals, such as moose, deer, and bears for their meat and hides.

(right) Seal was the Inuits' most important catch. They hunted from kayaks using harpoons.

Life of the Inuit

After abandoning Hudson, the mutineers stopped at Digges Island, in northern Hudson Bay, to try to get food from the Inuit people living there. Most of the Inuits' food supply was sea mammals, from which they also made bags, tools, weapons, and oil for lighting and cooking. In the summer, the Inuit tracked caribou herds for meat and hides.

Contact

The Inuit had few early contacts with Europeans. When Arctic explorer Martin Frobisher made contact with the Inuit of North America and Greenland in the late 1500s, he kidnapped one and took him back to England. The Inuit had no further contact until the Hudson's mutineers. The Inuit attacked the crew and several mutineers were killed in the fight.

(background) Surviving the cold Arctic climate is hard work. People must know how to find food and keep warm in winter, especially since help from neighbors might be miles away.

(right) The Inuit were very good hunters and fishers, as they lived in a land so cold that farming was not possible. They caught fish in winter through holes that they cut in the ice.

After Hudson

When the remaining eight mutineers returned to England, they were tried for the crime of mutiny. They were found not guilty, as the mutiny's leaders had died on the voyage. Rescue missions were sent to Hudson Bay, but they returned without Hudson.

The Search Continues

With the reports of what the crew had discovered in Hudson Bay, more expeditions were sent out to discover a passage to Asia. In 1612, the English formed the Company of the Merchants of London Discoverers of the Northwest Passage, or the Northwest Passage Company. The first expedition set out in 1612, again aboard the *Discovery*. The goals of this voyage were to find the passage and to look for Hudson. The voyage was not successful in finding Hudson or the passage.

Fur Trade

Around 1600, eleven years before Hudson's death, the French and English had begun trading furs with the native peoples around Hudson Bay. Beaver furs were the most valuable because the pelts were used to make felt hats that were very fashionable in Europe at the time. By 1670, the King of England had granted a charter, or trading monopoly, over the entire Hudson Bay area to a group of explorers and adventurers who became the Hudson's Bay Company.

Corsets

Whale bones were used to make lady's corsets. Historians estimate that in 200 years of whaling, 100,000 whales were killed at the Spitsbergen Islands.

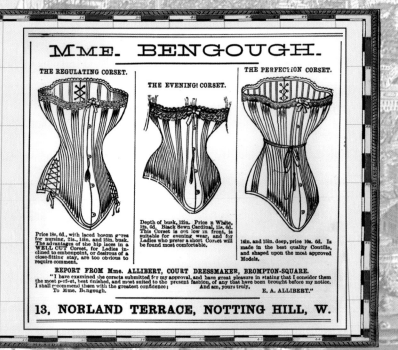

(background) Today, the Hudson River remains a busy port in present-day Manhattan, in New York City. Manhattan Island was purchased by the Dutch from the native peoples who originally lived there.

(below) Whales were such enormous animals that hunters had to work in teams in order to kill a single whale.

English Whaling

The Muscovy Company that hired Hudson for his first voyage was pleased with Hudson's discovery. When Hudson returned to England with reports of Whales Bay at Spitsbergen, the Muscovy Company sent out sailors to kill the whales. Whale blubber, or fat, was used to make soap, as fuel for burning in oil lamps, and as grease on carriage wheels. Hudson had been asked to lead the whaling expedition, but had declined because he wanted to continue looking for the passage to Asia.

(above) The beaver became extinct in Europe from over-hunting. By 1600, both English and French merchants came to Hudson Bay in search of valuable beaver pelts.

Dutch Colony

As a result of Hudson's third voyage, Dutch settlers were the first Europeans to colonize the area that is now New York City, which they called New Amsterdam. Thirty Dutch families established Fort Orange at present-day Albany, New York. The Dutch also purchased Manhattan Island from a native group for a mere $24. During the 1660s, the British, who had been living around the area, took over the Dutch colony and named it New York City.

The Native Way of Life

For the native peoples of North America, colonization by Europeans meant the end of their traditional way of life. When the European fur trade started, a huge number of animals were slaughtered for their pelts alone. Wasted animal meat meant that native families went hungry. European settlers also brought diseases, alcohol, and guns to the native peoples. Many native peoples were killed or pushed off their land after the Europeans arrived.

(below) Dutch settlers arrived at present-day Staten Island to establish a colony.

Warring Nations

Like most explorations, Hudson's voyages benefited the European countries he sailed for, but had terrible long-term effects on the native peoples. The Mahicans and Mohawks of the Hudson River were bitter rivals in the fur trade with the Dutch. This lead to a war between the two nations. The Mahicans were pushed off their land by the Mohawks, and later by European settlers.

(above) Fur traders arrive at a trading post of the Hudson Bay Company in boats and wagons.

- 1624 -

Dutch families establish Fort Orange.

- 1624 -

The Dutch purchase Manhattan Island from a group of native peoples.

- 1660 -

The British establish New York City.

Hudson's Legacy

Three hundred years after Hudson, an explorer from Norway named Roald Amundsen became the first person to sail through the Northwest and Northeast Passages. It took him three years to make the voyage.

The Passage

The geographers, explorers, merchants, and kings of the 1500s to the 1800s were wrong in thinking that the passage could be used for ships carrying cargo. Countless explorers from England, France, and the Netherlands had all searched for the passage. It was an enduring dream of explorers for hundreds of years. Although they did not find it, Henry Hudson, and the other explorers who tried, made startling discoveries about the lands and peoples that they encountered on their travels.

Hudson's Namesake

Henry Hudson and his crew were the first Europeans to successfully navigate the Hudson River, Hudson Strait, and Hudson Bay. The Hudson River allowed the Dutch to colonize the Hudson River Valley and establish New York City. Hudson's discoveries of the Hudson Strait and Hudson Bay, which he named Bay of God's Mercies, allowed later explorers to map the area. Eventually, this led English traders to move into the area.

What Happened to Hudson?

No one knows for certain what happened to Hudson after he was abandoned in Hudson Bay. Most likely, he died there, either from starvation or by drowning. Some people believe that Hudson made it to shore. They think he may have met some Cree native peoples who lived along the southern shore of Hudson Bay, and lived with them for the rest of his life.

(above) Norwegian explorer Roald Amundsen also explored the South Pole.

Legends and Ghosts

In the Catskill Mountains around the Hudson River in New York, there is a legend of the ghost of Henry Hudson. According to the legend, a band of ragged men roam the mountains playing a bowling game called ninepins that send sounds like thunder rolling down the mountains. The leader of the men is said to be the ghost of Henry Hudson.

(above right) The forests and temperate climate of New York were more pleasant than the surroundings on Hudson's Arctic voyages.

(background) The river named after Henry Hudson was called Muh-he-kun-ne-tuk by the Mahican people who used to live by its shores. The Hudson, that passes by New York, is also referred to as the North River today.

Glossary

ale A drink, similar to beer, made from malt, a grain, and the dried flowers of the hop plant

channel A body of water connecting two larger bodies of water, large enough for a ship to pass through

colony Territory that is ruled by another country

conspire To secretly plan together to do wrong

course The direction or path that a ship takes

financial support Money paid for a project

first mate On a ship, the person second in charge to the captain

flotilla A fleet of small boats

geographers People who study the physical features of the Earth, such as landforms, rivers, and mountains

gunner The crew member whose job it is to fire the guns

harpoon A spearlike weapon used to hunt whales and large fish

hoard To keep something to oneself so no one else can have it

infestation An outbreak or swarming of an unwanted pest

kayak A boat with a light wooden frame covered with watertight skins and propelled by a paddle

mash A mixture of food

mast A tall pole that supports the sails and rigging of a ship

merchant company A group of traders that pool their money and resources

merchant fleet A group of trading ships

monopoly Control over a product or service

mutiny The rebellion of crew members against their captain, often resulting in a takeover of the command of a ship

navigate To direct the course, or direction, of a ship

Northeast Passage A water route from the Atlantic Ocean through the Russian Arctic to the Pacific Ocean

Northwest Passage A water route from the Atlantic Ocean through the Canadian Arctic to the Pacific Ocean

porcelain A hard, white material made by baking clay

porthole A small, circular window in the side of a ship

seize To take by force

Spice Islands A group of islands of eastern Indonesia, also known as the Moluccas

subarctic The region just south of the Arctic

Virginia colony The colony established by the English in present-day Virginia

Index

1 2 3 4 5 6 7 8 9 0   Printed in the U.S.A.   4 3 2 1 0 9 8 7 6 5